SPANISH

for

surfers

olas

surfista

arrecife

dave
rearwin

SPANISH for SURFERS

Dave Rearwin

©2013

to
all those who dare
to
dream

Introduction & Author's note

If you've gone surfing abroad before, you're well aware that not everyone speaks English. Your next trip to a Spanish-speaking destination will be a lot more pleasant if you know at least a little Spanish, and it's an obvious advantage to target words and phrases you'll use in and around the surf zone. That's what this book is for. It contains over 500 words, expressions and images dealing with surf, surfing, and some of the other things you may need to communicate when you're on your own.

Be aware that in Spanish, much more than in English, the words used by surfers vary considerably from country to country, region to region, and place to place. What they say in Sayulita may not be what they say in Mazatlán or Tamarindo or Chile, and it is not possible to include everything here. But the words on this list should give you a starting point. Realize that especially in rural areas, native speakers won't be aware of the words used elsewhere, so if one word doesn't work, try another way of expressing what you want to say.

It's beyond the scope of this book to provide grammar, verb endings, and all the other detail that goes into speaking a language fluently. But pidgin Spanish is better than no Spanish, and most people will be happy that you gave it a go, and try to help you improve.

Since English has no masculine / feminine forms for "the" (*el, la, los, las*), make a bit of extra effort to learn which one goes with which noun.

● ● ●

NOTE: Most writers start sentences with capital letters and end them with periods (or other ending mark). For the sample sentences and phrases in this book, I gave this seemingly trivial issue a lot of thought. There's a lot of material in a small space here, and I wanted it to be as visuallly accessible as possible. I tried using traditional sentence format, but it was visually distracting. So I have settled on a mix: normal sentence format when it seemed necessary for clarity, a more telegraphic format (no capital letters and no punctuation) when the normal style seemed to get in the way. If this is a problem for you, please let me know via email. If enough people complain, I'll change it and publish a revised version. drwin808@gmail.com

Contents

Pronunciation

● All letters are always pronounced, except the letter h which is always silent.

● Except as noted, each letter is always pronounced the same way; the pronuciation doesn't change as it does in English.

● Two vowels together are each pronunced (not as in English words such as *bread, piece*, etc. where two vowels together are merged to have only one sound). But there is no pause or stop between vowels, the sound keeps flowing. NOT like English *uh-oh!* (for oops!), or *uh-huh* (for yes).

The pronunciation guide below gives a number of Spanish letters, each followed by the closest English sound. Letters not listed are pronounced as in English.

a: *father*   e: *café*   i: *machine*   o: *rope*   u: *flute*
h: (silent, never pronounced)
j: like very strong h in English (*La Jolla, CA*); ¡ajá! = *aha!*
ll: y (*La Jolla, CA*)
ñ: ny (*canyon*)
r: single quick tap of the tongue (sounds like American English tt in *I gotta go*)
rr: double tap of the tongue (like a little kid imitating a motorboat or car engine by going *rrrrrr, rrrrrr*)
s: always pronounced s, never a "z" sound.
v = b (voy sounds like *boy*); before u it sounds almost like a "w" (vuelo sounds like *way low*)
z = s (except in Spain, where z = th *with*)
ca, co, cu: like in English (*ka, ko, ku* sound); ce, ci = se, si
ch: *chop*
ga, go, gu: like in English (*ga, go, gu* sound); ge, gi: like a very strong h (*hey, he*) in English (same as Spanish j)
qu: like English k. NOT a "kw" sound as in *quick*.
k: does not exist in Spanish; sh: does not exist in Spanish – but you will see both used in recent language, especially on the internet.

Spanish words for pronunciation practice
You're going to see Spanish words every day—you can learn to pronounce them quickly and easily. Practice these samples (which tend to give gringos trouble) until they are second nature.

(Spanish word = closest English sound; NOT the meaning; **bold** = stress)
que = *K., Kay*
hay = *I., eye*
ay = *I., eye*
sí = *C, see*
ja, ja, ja = *ha, ha,ha* (actually does mean "ha, ha" as in laughing)
voy = *boy*
vez = base; **vec**es = **base** ace
hijo = *E. ho*
qué **hay** = *K.I.*
queso = *K. so*
Quito = **key** *toe*
hace = *ah say*
pa**gué** = *pa gay*
género = *hen arrow* (but with a Spanish r; stress on *hen*)
giro = *hero* (but with a Spanish r)
quién = *key N.*
qui**e**ro = *key arrow* (but with a Spanish r)
quince = *keen say*
cien = *C.N.*
ci**e**lo = *C.A. low*
hi**e**lo = *E.A. low*
vuelo = *way low*

ACCENT MARKS
An accent mark means that the accented letter is stressed. It makes a huge difference, so it's best to get it right.
p**a**go = I pay; pa**gó** = he/she paid
esta = this; est**á** = is
(There are differences of stress in English, as in *they prod**u**ce cars* and *the pr**o**duce section of the supermarket*, but they make less of a difference in terms of being understood.)

How do you say "is?"

This is a little tricky in Spanish. Without going into a lot of detail, here's what you say:

• *hay*: there is / there are (presence or existence of something): use *hay*

There are waves today = Hay olas hoy.
Are there a lot of people in the water? = ¿Hay mucha gente en el agua?
There's no time to call = No hay tiempo para llamar.
Is there any problem? = ¿Hay algún problema?
There's nothing better than a good ride. = No hay nada mejor que un buen recorrido.
There's nothing worse than this. = No hay nada peor que esto.
There's no hurry, there's no rush = No hay prisa.
No worries! = No hay cuidado.

• *estar*: Relative condition; location; action in progress: use *estar*

Condition:

It's wet / it's dry = está mojado / está seco
It's broken / it's fixed = está roto / está arreglado
It's dirty / it's clean = está sucio / está limpio
It's full / it's empty = está lleno / está vacío
Either it's open, or it's closed = o está abierto, o está cerrado
The water is cold / the water is warm = el agua está fria / el agua está tibia
The beer is cold / the coffee is hot = la cerveza está fría / el café está caliente
It's dark outside = está oscuro afuera
The sea is rough / The sea is smooth = el mar está revuelto / el mar está liso
The sea is choppy / The sea is glassy = el mar está picado / el mar está aceitoso

Location:

Where are the keys? = ¿Dónde están las llaves?

The airport is a long way from the city = el aeropuerto está muy lejos de la ciudad.*

*For locations, you also can use *queda*. For details, see the section *How to ask questions*.

Action in progress:

He's surfing = él está surfeando
They're running on the beach = ellos están corriendo en la playa
I'm talking to a friend = estoy hablando con un amigo

● *ser*: Identity, intrinsic quality* (this can be very subjective), ownership, time: use *ser*

Identity:

It's a whale / it's a shark = es una ballena / es un tiburón
I'm not American, I'm Canadian = no soy norteamericano, soy canadiense
It's not a crab, it's a lobster = no es un cangrejo, es una langosta

Intrinsic quality*:

This isn't so hard / it's quite easy = Esto no es tan difícil / es muy fácil
It's not necessary = No es necesario

Ownership:

It's not my suitcase = no es mi maleta
The suitcase is not mine = la maleta no es mía

Time:

What time is is now? = ¿Qué hora es ahora?
It's one o'clock = Es la una. / It's two o'clock = Son las dos.
What time is the party? = ¿A qué hora es la fiesta?
It's at three = Es a las tres.

*What's intrinsic quality?

Las olas son muy buenas en esta playa. = The waves are very good at this beach. (It's a good break, it usually has good waves, that's the way it is.)
Las olas están muy buenas hoy. = The waves are very good today. (This is a relative condition, or unusually good.)

La comida es muy buena. = The food is very good. (They serve good food there; it is of good quality; it's generally good.)
La comida está muy buena. = The food is very good. (This meal is a treat; the cook did a good job on it; it's even better than expected. If you compliment the cook, use *estar*.)

● *hacer*: Weather temperature: use *hacer*

What's the weather? / ¿Qué tiempo hace?
The weather is nice / hace buen tiempo
It's sunny = hace sol
It's hot / it's cold = hace calor / hace frío
It's very hot / it's very cold = hace mucho calor / hace mucho frío

● *hacer*: Time span up to now: use *hacer*

How long has it been = ¿Cuánto tiempo hace?
It's been a long time; it's been years = hace mucho tiempo; hace años
I haven't surfed for a week = hace una semana que no surfeo

Other expressions using *hacer*:

It's not necessary, there's no need = no hace falta
You don't have to shout = no hace falta gritar
It does damage =hace daño
That doesn't do any damage, that doesn't hurt anything = Eso no hace ningún daño.

Normally *hacer* means to do or to make:

He makes good boards = Él hace buenas tablas.

What do you do on weekends? = ¿Qué haces los fines de semana?
I don't do anything = no hago nada

● *tener*: Some common physical, mental and emotional states or sensations: use *tener*

I'm hot / I'm cold = tengo calor / tengo frío
I'm hungry / I'm thirsty = tengo hambre / tengo sed
I'm sleepy / I'm scared = tengo sueño / tengo miedo
I'm in a hurry / = tengo prisa
I feel like it / I don't feel like it = tengo ganas / no tengo ganas
I don't feel like going = no tengo ganas de ir; I don't feel like eating = no tengo ganas de comer
How old are you? = ¿Cuántos años tienes?; ¿Qué edad tienes?
 I'm 20 (years old) = tengo veinte años
Be careful = ten cuidado

Normally, *tener* means to have:

I have money, but I don't have time = tengo dinero, pero no tengo tiempo
I have a headache / I have a fever = tengo dolor de cabeza / tengo fiebre
I don't have a car = no tengo coche
I don't have any idea = no tengo ninguna idea

How it makes me feel

● *dar*: if something makes you hungry, thirsty, hot, cold, sleepy, scared (and a few others): use *dar*
It makes me hot / cold = me da calor / me da frío
It makes me hungry / thirsty = me da hambre / me da sed
It makes me sleepy / scared = me da sueño / me da miedo
It disgusts me = me da asco
Hurry up! = ¡Date prisa!
It makes me want to / it doesn't turn me on = me da ganas / no me da ganas
It makes me want to quit = me da ganas de parar
I don't feel like it = no me da la gana
he does whatever he feels like = hace lo que le da la gana

Normally, *dar* means to give:

Give me the keys = Dame las llaves.
I'm going to give you a pounding. = Te voy a dar una paliza.
That noise gives me a headache. = Ese ruido me da dolor de cabeza.

Notes

Words to live by

Every language has words that have multiple meanings. Learn to use the various meanings, and you can say a lot with a little. (This is how little kids get by—they don't know a lot of words, but the ones they know go a long way.) The words above are an example: although they make it a bit tricky at first, they can give you a broader range of expression.

Another use for *tener* and *hay* is necessity or obligation. *Tener* is person-specific (I have to, you have to); *hay* is general ("you" in the sense of "one" has to).

tener que = have to (person-specific)
hay que = have to (general)

Tengo que ir mañana = I have to go tomorrow
Tienes que ayudarme = you have to help me
Tenemos que estar en el aeropuerto para las cinco = We have to be at the airport by 5:00.

Hay que remar para coger olas = You have to paddle to catch waves (this doesn't mean you personally, but anyone)
Hay que llegar temprano = You have to get there early (one has to get there early, it's necessary to get there early)
Hay que llevar pasaporte = You have to carry a passport (one has to carry a passport, it's necessary to carry a passport)

The opposite of *hay que* is *no hace falta* or *no es necesario*

No hace falta llegar temprano = No es necesario llegar temprano = You don't have to get there early (one doesn't have to get there early)
No hace falta llevar pasaporte = No es necesario llevar pasaporte = You don't have to carry a passport (one doesn't have to carry a passport)

no hay que means you (generic) shouldn't, one shouldn't, it's not a good idea to

No hay que gritar = you shouldn't shout
No hay que tirar basura en la playa = you shouldn't throw trash on the beach

<u>Three words for "time"</u>

- time (measure) = el tiempo; it's been a long time = hace mucho tiempo; there's no time = no hay tiempo
- time (occurrence) = la vez; I went twice = fui dos veces; this time = esta vez; the other time = la otra vez; sometimes yes, sometimes no = a veces sí, a veces no
- time (of day) = la hora; ¿what time is it? = ¿qué hora es?; what time do you leave? = ¿a qué hora te vas?

<u>What the heck does *se* mean?</u>

For English speakers, the Spanish word *se* can be a headache—a real *dolor de cabeza*. Start by being aware of these three uses:

- Passive: basically, nobody did it, it just happened. It's the equivalent of English "it got..." as in it got broken, it got lost, it got misplaced.

Se rompió = it got broken, it broke
Se paró = it stopped (car, train, etc. – we aren't concerned with who stopped it)

- Reflexive: the person did it to him/herself. He cut himself, she burned herself, etc.

Se quemó = he/she burned himself/herself
Se cortó la mano = he/she cut his/her hand

- General: *se* means more or less "you" in the sense of "one" or "people"

¿Cómo se dice surfboard? = How do you say surfboard?
Se dice tabla = You say tabla.

Así se dice = that's how it's said, that's the way people say it

Eso no se dice = that isn't said, people don't say that (implies that you said something unacceptable, profane, insult, etc.)

¿Cómo se llama esto en castellano? = What do you call this in Spanish? What's this called in Spanish?
Se llama quilla. = It's called a fin.

In many cases you'll perceive considerable overlap; what matters is what people say. Grammar is just a way of trying to explain it. There are also quite a number of common verbs that are often used with *se* for no special reason. That's just the way it is.

Notes

Points of the compass; Amounts; Time of day

Directions
north = el norte; northeast = nordeste; northwest = noroeste
south = el sur; southeast = sudeste; southwest = suroeste
east = el este; northeast = nordeste; southeast = sudeste
west = el oeste; northwest = noroeste; southwest = suroeste
degrees (temperature, compass, angles) = grados

Prices are often given as in English: $3.99 = *"three ninety-nine"* = tres noventa y nueve, $3,99.
In most Spanish-speaking countries, a comma is used instead of a decimal point. *Point* = punto; *comma* = coma

100% = cien por ciento
50% = cincuenta por ciento
25% = veinte y cinco por ciento (veinticinco por ciento)
10% = diez por ciento
half = la mitad; double = doble; a quarter = un cuarto

Time of day is expressed with la (if one) or las (all other numbers). Minutes after the hour is expressed with "y" (and); minutes before the hour is expressed with *"menos"* (minus). The half hour is *"media"* (or *treinta*) and the quarter hour is *"cuarto"* (or *quince*).

1:00 = la una; 1:05 = la una y cinco; 1:30 = la una y media; 1:45 = las dos menos cuarto
3:00 = las tres; 3:15 = las tres y cuarto; 3:25 = las tres y veinticinco; 3:50 = las cuatro menos diez

noon = mediodía; midnight = medianoche
morning = la mañana; afternoon = la tarde; evening, night = la noche
the crack of dawn = la madrugada

day = el día; week = la semana; month = el mes; year = el año

once = una vez
twice = dos veces
 three times = tres veces
many times = muchas veces
 a couple of times = un par de veces

at times = a veces
sometimes = algunas veces
sometime = alguna vez

500+ Words, expressions & images

a closeout = un cerradón, una ola cerrada

a little / a lot = poco, un poco / mucho; a little more = un poco más; a little less = un poco menos; a little bigger = un poco más grande; a lot bigger = mucho más grande; a lot more = mucho más

after / before / during = después / antes / durante

aggro = agro, agresivo; that guy is really aggro = ese tipo es muy agro

all = todo; all day = todo el día; all night = toda la noche; all the waves = todas las olas; all the surfers = todos los surfistas; either all or nothing = o todo o nada

alone / together = solo / juntos; I prefer to surf alone = prefiero surfear solo

along = a lo largo de; along the coast = a lo largo de la costa

already / not anymore / still / not yet = ya / ya no / todavía / todavía no

always / sometimes / some time / never = siempre / a veces / alguna vez / nunca

ankle = el tobillo

arm = el brazo

arrive, get here, get there / depart, leave = llegar / salir, partir

arrivals / departures = las llegadas / las salidas

at an angle / straight = en ángulo / recto, derecho

at what time = a qué hora; what time are you leaving = ¿a qué hora te vas?

back (person; wave) = la espalda

backside / frontside = backside, de espaldas a la ola / frontside, de cara a la ola

backward / forward = hacia atrás / hacia adelante

backward, reversed = al revés

backwash = la contraola; la resaca

bad / good = malo / bueno

bandage = la venda; this bandage is not clean = esta venda no está limpia

bar, sand bar = el bajo, la barra, el banco de arena

barrel = el barrel, el tubo, el barril

beach = la playa

beach break = rompiente con fondo de arena

because = porque; just because = porque sí

before / after / during = antes / después / durante

bend = doblar; you have to bend your knees = hay que doblar las rodillas

beside = al lado de, junto a; it breaks beside a jetty = rompe al lado de un
muelle

UNA IZQUIERDA BACKSIDE – VOCABULARIO

el labio = lip; el hueco = hollow, the pocket; el brazo = shoulder of a wave
(usually means *arm*); agarrar = to grab, to grip, to hold onto; el canto = the
edge, the rail (board); con = with; la mano = hand; derecho/a = right (not
left); izquierda = left; debajo = below, under; dentro = inside, in

---

better / worse = mejor / peor; much better = mucho mejor; not much better
= no mucho mejor; a little better = un poco mejor

big = grande; bigger = más grande; very big = muy grande; not so big = no tan
grande; this big = así de grande; the bigger the wave, the more power it
has = cuanto más grande la ola, más potencia tiene

bill (to be paid) = la cuenta, la factura

bill (money) = el billete; a $20 bill = un billete de veinte dólares

bite = morder; it bit me = me mordió; that dog doesn't bite = ese perro no muerde

blank (surfboard) = el foam

bleed = sangrar; you're bleeding = estás sangrando

blood = la sangre; a lot of blood = mucha sangre; there is blood in the water = hay sangre en el agua

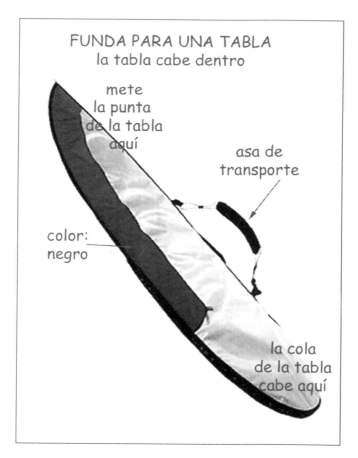

FUNDA PARA UNA TABLA
la tabla cabe dentro

mete la punta de la tabla aquí

asa de transporte

color: negro

la cola de la tabla cabe aquí

LA FUNDA– VOCABULARIO

la funda = the bag, soft case; para = for; la tabla = the surfboard; caber = fit, fit inside; dentro = inside; meter = put in; la punta = the nose (board); aquí = here; el asa = the handle; el transporte = transport, carrying; el color = color; negro = black; la cola = the tail

board bag = la funda

board, surfboard = la tabla

boat = el barco; la lancha; la panga; let's go by boat = vamos en lancha; we're going by boat = vamos en lancha

bodysurfing = bodysurfing; surfear sin tabla, nadando

boil (reef) = la ebullición; el hervidero; el remolino

bomb = la bomba; ola grande; he caught a bomb = cogió una bomba

el mar: liso

alga marina

la espuma: blanca

la pared: vertical

la estela de la tabla

quilla

alma

UN BOTTOM BACKSIDE
(giro abajo, espaldas a la ola)

UN BOTTOM BACKSIDE – VOCABULARIO

el bottom = bottom turn; el mar = the sea; liso = smooth, glassy; el alga marina = seaweed, kelp; la espuma = the foam; blanco = white; la pared = the wall; vertical = vertical; la estela = the wake (of board, boat, etc.); la quilla = the fin (board), keel; el alma = the stringer (board), the heart; el giro = the turn; abajo = below; la espalda = the back (person); la ola = the wave

---

bone = el hueso

booties = los botines; los escarpines

bottle = la botella; the bottle is half empty / but the glass is half full = la
botella está medio vacía / pero el vaso está medio lleno

bottom = el fondo; sand bottom = el fondo de arena; rock bottom = fondo de
piedra

bottom turn = el bottom turn, giro en la parte más baja de la ola

break (surf) = la rompiente, el break

el cielo está azul

gaviota

turistas

rompeolas

playa de arena

arrecife

cormoranes

MAR PLATO -
NO HAY OLAS

MAR PLATO; NO HAY OLAS - VOCABULARIO

el cielo = the sky; azul = blue los turistas = tourists; el rompeolas = the
breakwater; la gaviota = the seagull; la playa = the beach; la arena = the sand;
el cormorán = the cormorant; el arrecife = the reef; el mar = the sea; plato =
flat as a plate; hay = there is; la ola = the wave

---

break = romper; the waves break = las olas rompen; the wave breaks = la ola
rompe; it broke in front of me = rompió delante de mí; someone broke a
bottle on the beach = alguien rompió una botella en la playa; it breaks
hard = rompe muy recio

break, fracture (bone) = le fracturó el brazo = it broke his arm

bring / take = traer / llevar; bring some wax = trae parafina; I'm bringing two
   boards = traigo dos tablas

broken = roto; it's broken =está roto; this is broken = esto está roto

broken, fractured (bone) = the bone is broken = el hueso está fracturado

breathe = respirar; you can't breathe underwater = no se puede respirar
   debajo del agua

breathing = la respiración; hold your breath = contener la respiración; how
   long can you hold your breath? = ¿por cuanto tiempo puedes contener la
   respiración?

bumpy = bacheado; it's very bumpy = está muy bacheado

burn = quemar; I burned myself = me quemé; they burn the trash outside =
   queman la basura afuera

burn = la quemadura; it's a serious burn = es una quemadura grave

buy = comprar; where can I buy it = ¿en dónde puedo comprarlo?

calf (leg) = la pantorrilla; I have a cramp in my calf = me está dando un
   calambre en la pantorrilla

call = llamar; call the police = llama a la policia; call a lifguard = llama a un
   salvavidas; call a doctor = llama a un médico

can, tin = el bote, la lata; a can of beer = un bote de cerveza; a can of
   sardines = una lata de sardinas

can, able to = poder; I can't = no puedo; I can't surf today because I have to
   work = no puedo surfear hoy porque tengo que trabajar

catch = agarrar, coger; catch a wave = agarrar una ola, coger una ola

cheap / expensive = barato / caro; cheaper = más barato; very cheap = muy
   barato

choppy = picado, chopy; the sea is very choppy = el mar está muy picado

clean / dirty = limpio / sucio; the room is very clean = el cuarto está muy
   limpio; the beach is dirty = la playa está sucia

cleanup set = la escoba, la barredora; la última barredora acabó con todos =
   the last cleanup set finished off everybody

cliff = el acantilado; someone fell off the cliff = alguien se cayó del acantilado;
   jump off the cliff = saltar del acantilado

close, close to to, near = cerca; it's very close = está muy cerca; it's close to
   the beach = está cerca de la playa

close out = cerrarse; the wave closed out on me = se me cerró la ola

closeouts = cerradas

close / open = cerrar / abrir; it's closed = está cerrado; what time does the
   store close = ¿a qué hora cierra la tienda?

el labio (el codo)

la pared está
vertical y hueca

el surfista

OLA CERRADA
no es posible seguir adelante

UNA OLA CERRADA – VOCABULARIO

el surfista = the surfer; el labio = the lip (also for people); el codo = the lip (wave), elbow (people); la pared = the wall; vertical = vertical; y = and; hueco = hollow; la ola = the wave; cerrado/a = closed; no es posible = it's not possible; seguir = follow, continue; adelante = ahead, forward

---

clothes, clothing = la ropa

cold / hot = frío / caliente; the beer is not cold = la cerveza no está fría; the water is cold = el agua está fría

come / go = venir / ir

come back, return / go back = regresar, volver

come down / go down = bajar; the drop is when you go down the face of the wave = la bajada es cuando bajas la cara de la ola

come in / go in = entrar

come out / go out = salir

come up / go up = subir; go up the face = sube la cara (de la ola)

continue, keep going / stop = seguir, continuar / parar; keep going along this road = sigue por este camino; follow the river = sigue el río; do you follow me = ¿me sigues?

coral = el coral; a coral bottom = un fondo de coral; a coral reef = un arrecife de coral

cost = costar; how much does it cost = ¿cuánto cuesta?

couple (pair) = el par; a couple of times = un par de veces; you got yourself a couple of nice waves = te agarraste un par de buenas olas; we'll be here a couple more weeks = vamos a estar aquí un par de semanas más; it takes a couple of hours = toma un par de horas

cramp = el calambre; I have a cramp in my right leg = me ha dado un calambre en la pierna derecha

cranking = cocinando (cooking); it's cranking today = está cocinando hoy

crest / trough = la cresta / el valle, el seno; the height of the wave is measured from trough to crest = la altura de la ola se mide del valle a la cresta

cross = cruzar, atravesar; cross the street here = cruza la calle aquí; go across the face = atravesar la cara (de la ola)

current = la corriente; there's a lot of current = hay mucha corriente

cut back = cut back; recortar

cut = cortar; it cut me = me cortó; I cut my foot = me corté el pie; he cut his foot = se cortó el pie

damage / damaged = dañar / dañado; my board is damaged = mi tabla está dañada

damage = el daño (often used in plural); there's no serious damage = no hay daños graves; that won't hurt you = eso no te hace daño

day after tomorrow / day before yesterday = pasado mañana / anteayer

deck = el deck, la superficie superior de la tabla

deep* = profundo; deep water = agua profunda; it's not very deep = no es muy profunda (*there is no common Spanish word meaning shallow; you have to say "not deep")

degrees (temperature, compass, angles) = grados; the water is 20 degrees = el agua está a veinte grados; the swell is hitting from 220° = el swell pega de doscientos veinte grados

departures / arrivals = las salidas / las llegadas

different / similar / equal, same = diferente / parecido / igual

ding = agujero, abolladura; there's a ding on the rail = hay una abolladura en el canto

dirty / clean = sucio / limpio; this glass is dirty = este vaso está sucio; the sand is dirty = la arena está sucia; the water is dirty = el agua está sucia

disorganized (swell) / organized = desordenado, revuelto / ordenado

la torre de salvavidas — el cielo — las nubes — la rompiente — el rompeolas — la sombra de un edifício — la contraola — roca o arrecife — hay mucha espuma blanca — EL MAR ESTÁ REVUELTO

EL MAR ESTÁ REVUELTO – VOCABULARIO

la torre = the tower; el salvavidas = the lifeguard; el rompeolas = the breakwater; el cielo = the sky; la nube = the cloud; la rompiente = the break, the breaking wave; la sombra = the shadow, shade; el edifício = the building la contraola = the backwash; la roca = the rock; o = or; el arrecife = the reef; hay = there is; mucho = much, a lot of; la espuma = the foam; blanco/a = white

---

dive (skin/SCUBA) = bucear; hacer pesca submarina

diving (skin/SCUBA) = el buceo; la pesca submarina

dive (into the water) = zambullirse, tirarse de cabeza

dive (under the water from the surface) = sumergirse

diver (skin/SCUBA, etc.) = el buzo

door / window = la puerta / la ventana; the door's open but the window isn't = la puerta está abierta pero la ventana no

down = abajo = down the street = calle abajo; farther down = más abajo

drink / eat = tomar, beber / comer; what are you going to drink = ¿qué vas a tomar?; aren't you going to eat =¿no vas a comer?

drive = conducir, manejar; who's going to drive? = ¿quién va a manejar? ¿quién va a conducir?

drop (surfing) = la bajada; a steep drop = una bajada muy inclinada; nice drop = buena bajada

drop in (snake) = dropear, dar un cañoneo; hacer una saltada; hacer una intromisión

UN CAÑONEO – VOCABULARIO

el labio = lip; el hueco = hollow, the pocket; agachado = crouched, in a crouch; la cabeza = head; vacío = empty; el surfista = surfer; corriendo = running, riding a wave; dropear, dropeando = dropping in (on another surfer); la ebullición = (reef) boil; el cañoneo = the drop-in (on another surfer)

---

drown = ahogarse; he almost drowned = por poco se ahoga

drunk = tomado, borracho; he's really drunk = está muy borracho (está muy tomado) duck dive = hacer pato, hacer cuchara, filtrar; with a longboard it's hard to duck dive = con tablón es difícil hacer pato; you duck dive to get through the break = se hace pato para pasar la rompiente

during / before / after = durante / antes / después

ear (inner) = el oído; I can't take the pressure in my ears = no aguanto la presión en los oídos

ear (external) = la oreja

early = temprano; earlier = más temprano; very early = muy temprano

eat / drink = comer / beber, tomar

easy / hard = fácil / difícil; that is hard but this is harder = eso es difícil, pero esto es más difícil

eddy, whirlpool = el remolino

elbow = el codo; I hurt my elbow = me lastimé el codo

empty / full = vacío / lleno

end, be over = acabarse, terminar; it's already over = ya se acabó; it already ended = ya terminó

entrance / exit = la entrada / la salida; where's the exit = ¿dónde está la salida?; there's no way out = no hay salida

equal, same / similar / different = igual / parecido / diferente; it's all the same to me (I don't care) = me da igual

equipment / team = el equipo / el equipo

everything / nothing / something = todo / nada / algo; everything is very good = todo está muy bueno

exit / entrance = la salida / la entrada

expensive / cheap = caro / barato; very expensive = muy caro; not so expensive = no tan caro

face (wave, person) = la cara

fall = caer; I fell = me caí; fall = la caída; a fall = una caída

far, far away / near = lejos / cerca; it's not far = no está lejos; it's a long way away = está muy lejos

fast / slow = rápido / despacio

fetch = el alcance, distancia en mar abierto sobre la cual el viento sopla sin obstáculo

fiberglass = la fibra de vidrio

fin (surboard) = la quilla; boards have from one to 5 fins = las tablas tienen entre una y cinco quillas

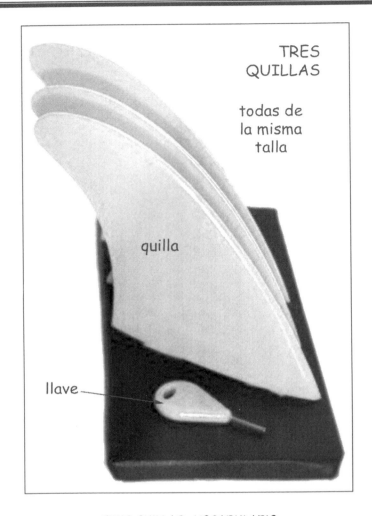

TRES
QUILLAS

todas de
la misma
talla

quilla

llave

TRES QUILLAS –VOCABULARIO

tres = three; la quilla = the fin; todas = all; mismo/a = same; la talla = the size, the cut; la llave = the key

---

fins (fish; SCUBA) = las aletas; for bodysurfing you need fins = para el bodysurf necesitas aletas

find / lose = encontrar, hallar / perder; where did you find that? = ¿dónde encontraste eso?

finger = el dedo

fingernail = la uña

finish, end / start, begin = terminar, acabar / empezar; what time does it end = ¿a qué hora termina?

fish / to fish / fishing = el pescado / pescar / la pesca; do you like fishing? = ¿te gusta la pesca?

UNA CAÍDA DE CABEZA – VOCABULARIO:

la punta = the nose (board), tip, point; de = of; la tabla = the surfboard; el traje = the suit; el neopreno = neoprene, a wetsuit; la manga = the sleeve; corto/a = short; la cara = the face (wave; people); vertical = vertical; la caída = the fall; de cabeza = head first; para abajo = downward

---

first / last / next = primero / último / próximo; who's going first? = ¿quién va primero?; this is my last wave = ésta es mi última ola; I'm going to take the next wave all the way in = voy a tomar la próxima ola hasta la orilla fix, repair = arreglar; by when can you fix it = ¿para cuándo lo puedes arreglar?

flat / bumpy = llano, plato / bacheado

float / sink = flotar / hundir; it floats well = flota bien; the tail sinks = la cola se hunde

flotation = la flotación

fly / take off (airplane) / land = volar / despegar / aterrizar

flight = el vuelo; what time is the flight? = ¿a qué hora es el vuelo?

foam = el foam (surboard only), la espuma

follow / lead = seguir / conducir, llevar

food / beverage, drink(s) = la comida / la bebida

foot = el pie

forearm = el antebrazo

forward / back = adelante / atrás

from / to / until = de / a / hasta; from 9 to 5 = de nueve a cinco; until midnight = hasta medianoche

frontside / backside = frontside, de cara a la ola / backside, de espaldas a la ola

fill / to empty = llenar / vaciar; let's fill the tank = vamos a llenar el tanque

full / empy = lleno / vacío; the tank is full = el tanque está lleno

get = conseguir, obtener, coger

get there, get here, arrive = llegar; what time do we get there? = ¿a qué hora llegamos?; what time does the flight get in? = ¿a qué hora llega el vuelo?

get in / get out = entrar / salir; remontar (surfing); you get out through this door = se sale por esta puerta; it's hard to get out on big days = es difícil remontar en días de oleaje fuerte

get through the wave (going out) = pasar la ola, pinchar la ola; with a short board you can get through the waves by duck diving = con tabla corta se puede pasar las olas haciendo pato

give = dar; give me = dame; deme (more formal)

give a gift, give away = regalar

glass (substance) = el vidrio; there's broken glass in the sand = hay vidrio roto en la arena

glass (for drinking) = el vaso; the glass is half full = el vaso está medio lleno / but the bottle is half empty = pero la botella está medio vacía

glassy = mar aceitoso, mar liso, mar de aceite, glasy; it's glassy = el mar está muy liso

glove = el guante; I don't use gloves to dive = no uso guantes para bucear go / stay = ir / quedar(se); where are you going? = ¿adónde vas?; I'm going to buy some wax = voy a comprar parafina

go (back) out (past the break) = remontar; it's easier to go out through the channel = es más fácil remontar por el canal

go back, return = volver, regresar: when do you go back? = ¿cuándo regresas?

go down = bajar; go down the face = bajar la cara

go in, get in = entrar; does one go in through this door = ¿se entra por esta puerta?

go out, get out = salir; how does one go out = ¿cómo se sale?

go up = subir; go up the face = subir la cara

go = ir; where are you going = ¿adónde vas?; who are you going with = ¿con quién vas?; are you going to surf = ¿vas a surfear?

good / bad = bueno / malo; very good = muy bueno; not very good = no muy bueno

goofy-foot = goofy

grab, grip, hold on = agarrar, el agarre; hang onto the board! = ¡agárrate a la tabla!; esta quilla da mucho agarre en los giros = this fin gives a lot of grip in the turns (holds well in turns)

gremmie = gremmie

ground swell = mar de fondo; 20-second ground swell = mar de veinte segundos, swell de veinte segundos

gun (big wave board) = el gun, el pincho

hace falta = it's necessary; no hace falta = there's no need, it's not necessary

hand = la mano; I cut my hand = me corté la mano; I burned my hand = me quemé la mano

handle, take, hold up under; it handles a big swell = aguanta swell de grand tamaño; I can't take a lot of pressure in my ears = no aguanto mucha presión en los oídos

hangover = resaca; crudo; I have a hangover = tengo resaca; I'm hung over = estoy crudo

hard, difficult = difícil; this peak is hard to ride = este pico es difícil de correr; it's a difficult drop = es una bajada difícil

hard (not soft) = duro

have = tener; I don't have that much time = no tengo tanto tiempo

have to (generic) = hay que; you have to paddle hard = hay que remar fuerte; you have to practice = hay que practicar

head = la cabeza; my head hurts = me duele la cabeza

heat = el calor; I feel hot = tengo calor; aren't you hot = ¿no tienes calor?; it's hot today = hace calor hoy

hear = oir; I don't hear anything = no oigo nada; oye = listen!

heavy / light = pesado / ligero; it's a very heavy wave = es una ola muy pesada; this board is very heavy = esta tabla es muy pesada

height = la altura

help = ayudar; I'll help you = yo te ayudo; will you help me with this? = ¿me ayudas con esto? Help! = ¡Socorro!

here = aquí; around here = por aquí; is there a market around here = ¿hay un mercado por aquí?

high tide / low tide = el pleamar, la marea alta, la marea llena / la marea baja, la marea seca

high / low = alto /bajo; higher / lower = más alto / más bajo; very high / very low = muy alto / muy bajo

higher (location) / lower (location) = más alto, más arriba / más bajo, más abajo

hit = pegar, golpear; did the board hit you = ¿te pegó la tabla?

hold on, grip = agarrar; you have to hold onto the board = hay que agarrar la tabla

hole = el hoyo, el agujero; el hueco

hollow = hueco/a; el hueco; the waves are very hollow = la olas están muy huecas

hope, expect = esperar; I hope so = espero que sí; I expect to go next year = espero ir el año que viene

hot / cold = caliente / frio; the coffee is hot = el café está caliente; the ocean is still cold = el mar está frío todavía

hour / minute / second = la hora / el minuto / el segundo

how big = ¿de qué tamaño?; ¿qué tan grande?; how big are the waves = ¿de qué tamaño son las olas?

how far = ¿a qué distancia?; ¿qué tan lejos?

how long (time) = ¿cuánto tiempo?; how long do you need? = ¿cuánto tiempo necesitas?

how many = ¿cuántos?; how many feet = ¿cuántos pies?; how many km = ¿cuántos kilómetros?; how many miles = ¿cuántas millas?; how many hours = ¿cuántas horas?; how many times = ¿cuántas veces?

how much = ¿cuánto?; how much does it cost? = ¿cuánto cuesta?

how = ¿cómo?; how are you = ¿cómo estás?

UN BUEN SPOT CON MAREA LLENA

hay picos surfeables

1 a 2 metros de agua

CON MAREA SECA NO SIRVE

no hay olas

pura piedra

ocho horas después

quedan
unos charcos

CON MAREA LLENA O SECA – VOCABULARIO

bueno = good; el spot = the surf spot; con = with; la marea = the tide; llena = full, high tide; hay = there is, there are; el pico = the peak; surfeable = surfable; el metro = the meter (about 1.1 yards or 3.3 feet, 39.37 inches); el agua = the water; seco = dry, low tide; servir = to serve, to be useable;

puro/a = pure, nothing but; la piedra = the rock; ocho = eight; la hora = the hour; después = later, after; quedar = to stay, to remain; unos/unas = some, a few; el charco = the pool, the puddle

---

hunger = el hambre; I'm hungry = tengo hambre; I'm very hungry = tengo mucha hambre; I'm not hungry = no tengo hambre

hurricane = el huracán

hurry = apresurarse, apurarse, darse prisa; hurry! ¡apúrate!, ¡date prisa!

hurt, be painful = doler; my arm hurts = me duele el brazo; where does it hurt? = ¿dónde te duele?

hurt, injure = lastimar; he got hurt = se lastimó

ice = el hielo; there's no ice = no hay hielo; where do they sell ice? = ¿dónde se vende hielo?

in a while = al rato; we'll go in a while = al rato nos vamos

inside = adentro; it breaks farther inside = cae más adentro

jellyfish = el aguamar; la aguaviva; watch out for jellyfish = cuidado con los aguamares

jetty, breakwater = la escollera, el rompeolas; there's a right that comes off the jetty = hay una derecha que abre de la escollera

jetty, pier = el muelle

jump = saltar; he jumped off the board = saltó de la tabla

keep going, continue / stop = seguir / parar; keep going = sigue; stop here = para aquí

kelp = el alga marina

knee = la rodilla

knot (in rope; kt) = el nudo; there's a knot in my leash = hay un nudo en mi invento

know = saber; I don't know = no sé; I don't know how to swim = no sé nadar; do you know the way = ¿sabes el camino?; who knows = ¿quién sabe?

know = conocer (be familiar with); I don't know that brand = no conozco esa marca; I know her = la conozco; do you know that guy? = ¿conoces a aquel tipo?

kook = papa, patata; madero, made; tronco; that kook ran over me = ese madero me atropelló

lacking, short; missing = faltar; we're short $10 = nos faltan diez dólares; there's $20 missing = faltan veinte dólares; we have 30k to go = nos faltan treinta kilómetros para llegar

landing = el aterrizaje; nice landing = buen aterrizaje

large = grande; más grande

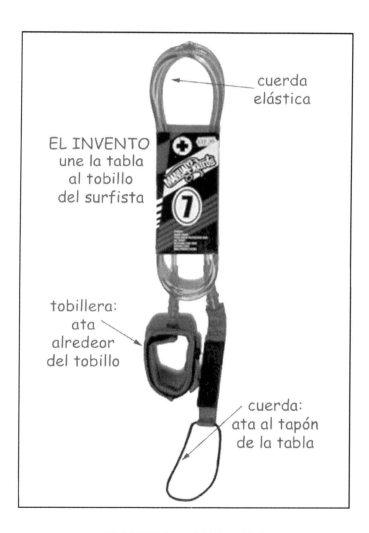

cuerda
elástica

EL INVENTO
une la tabla
al tobillo
del surfista

tobillera:
ata
alredeor
del tobillo

cuerda:
ata al tapón
de la tabla

EL INVENTO – VOCABULARIO

el invento = the leash (board); unir = join, connect, unite; la tabla = the surfboard; el tobillo = the ankle; el surfista = the surfer; la cuerda = the cord; elástico/a = elastic; la tobillera = the ankle strap; atar = tie; alrededor = around; el tapón = the plug

last = durar; the big swells don't last long = los swells (oleajes) grandes no duran mucho

last / first / next = primero / último / próximo; the last wave of the set is the biggest = la última ola de la serie es la más grande; I'm going to take the next wave all the way in = voy a tomar la próxima ola hasta la orilla; first you have to catch it = primero tienes que cogerla

late = tarde; later = más tarde; very late = muy tarde

leash = el invento, el lish, la cuerda, la pita; my leash broke = se me rompió el lish; he surfs without a leash = él surfea sin pita

leave / take = dejar / tomar; leave the money on the table = deja el dinero en la mesa

leave / take along = dejar / llevar; we didn't take him to the beach, we left him = no lo llevamos a la playa, lo dejamos

left = izquierda; this wave is a left = esta ola abre a la izquierda; esta ola es una izquierda

left, left over = quedar; there's no wax left = no queda parafina; there's no time left = no queda tiempo; I only have $20 left = me quedan sólo veinte dólares

left over, surplus = there are three extra tickets = sobran tres boletos; there's one person too many = sobra una persona

leg = la pierna; my right leg hurts = me duele la pierna derecha

less, fewer = menos; less expensive = menos caro; it costs less = cuesta menos; fewer waves = menos olas; fewer surfers = menos surfistas

let go = soltar; he let go of the board = él soltó la tabla; let go! = ¡suelta!

lifeguard = el salvavidas, la salvavidas (female guard); there's no lifeguard on this beach = no hay salvavidas en esta playa

light / heavy = ligero / pesado; my old board is a lot heavier = mi tabla antigua es mucho más pesada

light / dark = claro / oscuro

light = la luz; there's no light = no hay luz

like = como; I want one like that one = quiero uno como aquel

like: I like it = me gusta; do you like it = ¿te gusta?; don't you like it = ¿no te gusta?

lined up = alineado

lineup = el lineup; el pico; donde se espera la llegada de una ola; grupo de surfistas que esperan la llegada de una ola

lip (person or wave) = el labio

lip = el labio, el codo (of wave); the lip hit me and I fell off the board = me pegó el labio y me caí de la tabla

a little / a lot = un poco / mucho; a little more = un poco más; a little less = un poco menos; a little better = un poco mejor

a lot / a little = mucho / un poco; a lot less = mucho menos; a lot more = mucho más; a lot better = mucho mejor

long / short = largo / corto; long period swell = swell de período largo; short period swell = swell de período corto

longboard = la tabla larga, un tablón, un longboard

look, look at / see = mirar / ver; what are you looking at = ¿qué miras?; what do you see = ¿qué ves?

look for / find = buscar / encontrar; what are you looking for = ¿qué buscas?; I can't find it = no lo encuentro

lose / look for / find = perder / buscar / encontrar; I lost it, but I found it = lo perdí, pero lo encontré

lost = perdido

low / high = bajo / alto; lower = más bajo; very low = muy bajo

lower down, farther down (location) / higher up = más bajo; más abajo / más arriba

many / few = muchos / pocos; many more = muchos más; there are not a lot of surfable waves = no hay muchas olas surfeables

mask = la máscara; I need a diving mask = necesito una máscara de buceo

measure = medir; how do you measure the height of a wave? = ¿cómo se mide la altura de una ola?; in Hawai'i they measure by the back = en Hawái se mide por la espalda

medium = medio

messed up (swell, ocean) = desfasado

mine / yours / his = mío / tuyo / suyo (de él); it's mine = es mío; it's not mine, it's yours = no es mío, es tuyo

minute / second / hour = el minuto / el segundo / la hora

missing = perdido, extraviado, que falta; there's twenty dollars missing = faltan veinte dólares; there's a screw missing = falta un tornillo

money = el dinero; give me the money = dame el dinero

more / less = más / menos; more or less = más o menos; the more the better = cuanto más, mejor; the more you eat, the more you want = cuanto más comes, más quieres

much / a little = mucho / poco; much more = mucho más; much less = mucho menos

muscle = el músculo

mushy (wave) = aguada, fofa, sin fuerza

near, close to / far = cerca / lejos; it's very close = está muy cerca; it's near the beach = está cerca de la playa

necessary = es necesario; hace falta

neck / throat = el cuello / la garganta

need = necesitar; what do you need? = ¿qué necesitas?; I need a leash = necesito un invento; how many do you need? = ¿cuántos necesitas?

new / old = nuevo / viejo, antiguo

newbie / expert = novato / experto, veterano

el mar está liso; no hay viento

pared inclinada

estela de la tabla

CORRER EN LA PUNTA DE LA TABLA

CORRER EN LA PUNTA DE LA TABLA – VOCABULARIO

el mar = the sea; está = is; liso/a = smooth; hay = there is; el viento = wind; la pared = wall; inclinado/a = steep; correr = run, ride a wave; la punta = nose (of surfboard), point, tip; la tabla = surfboard; la estela = wake (boat, surfboard) next to = al lado de, junto a

next / first / last = próximo / primero / último; the next time I'll bring the other board = la próxima vez traigo la otra tabla; this is the first and last time I surf with him = ésta es la primera y última vez que surfeo con él

none / all = ninguno / todos = none of them knows how to surf = ninguno de ellos sabe surfear; all of them are going = todos ellos van

nose (board) / tail = la punta / la cola

nose (person) = la nariz; I have a broken nose = tengo la nariz fracturada

nose ride = correr una ola estando muy cerca de la punta de la tabla

not necessary = no es necesario; no hace falta

nobody, no one / somebody, someone / everybody, everyone = nadie / alguien / todos

nothing / something / everything = nada / algo / todo

nowhere / somewhere / everywhere = en ninguna parte / en alguna parte / en todas partes

ocean = el océano; the Pacific Ocean = el Océano Pacífico; the Atlantic Ocean = el Océano Atlántico

offshore wind / onshore wind = viento terral / viento marero, viento maral

oil / oily; glassy (ocean) = el aceite / aceitoso

old / new = viejo, antiguo / nuevo

old / young = viejo / joven

on a high tide = con marea llena

on a low tide = con marea seca

on a north swell = con swell (del) norte

on a sound swell = con swell (del) sur

on a west swell = con swell (del) oeste

on an east swell = con swell (del) este

on time / late = a tiempo / con retraso

once, one time / twice, two times = una vez / dos veces

only = sólo, solamente

onshore wind / offshore wind = viento marero; viento maral / viento terral

open = abrir; it's open = está abierto; what time does it open = ¿a qué hora abre?

organized / disorganized = ordenado / desordenado

other / same = otro / mismo; it's another board = es otra tabla; that's something else = eso es otra cosa

outside / inside = afuera / adentro

over, end = acabarse; this will end soon = esto se acaba pronto; it's all over =
se acabó; the party's over = se acabó la fiesta

over, above / under, below = encima de, sobre / debajo de, bajo

owe = deber; how much do I owe you = ¿cuánto le debo?; you owe me 200
pesos = me debes doscientos pesos; I don't owe you anything = no le
debo nada

paddle out = remontar

paddle = remar; you have to paddle hard = hay que remar fuerte

el mar está
un poco picado

espray
del viento
terral

cara un poco
bacheada

UNA BUENA DERECHA
pero bacheada por
la marea llena y resaca

UNA BUENA DERECHA, PERO BACHEADA – VOCABULARIO

el mar = the sea; un poco = a little, a bit; picado/a = chopppy; la cara = the
face (person or wave); bacheado/a = bumpy; el espray = spray; el viento =
the wind; terral = offshore; bueno/a = good; derecha = a right; pero = but; la
marea llena = the high tide; la resaca = the backwash

---

pay = pagar; I paid already = ya pagué

peak = el pico; this peak isn't for newbies = este pico no es para novatos

surfista de tabla de remo remontando
labio
surfista arrancando
cresta
estela
remo
cara
brazo
surfista ya corriendo la ola
espuma
PICO
abre a izquierda y a derecha

UN PICO A IZQUIERDA Y A DERECHA – VOCABULARIO

el surfista = the surfer; la tabla de remo = SUP board; remontar = go (back) out, go up over the wave; el remo = the paddle, the oar; arrancar = to start, to take off; la cara = the face (wave or person); la cresta = the crest; el labio = the lip (wave or person); la estela = the wake (boat or board); el brazo = the shoulder (wave), arm (person); correr = to run, to ride a wave; la ola = the wave; la espuma = the foam; el pico =the peak; abrir = to open; la izquierda = left; la derecha = right; abre a izquierda = you can go left, the left is open; arrancando = taking off; remontando = going (back) out; corriendo = running, riding (a wave)

---

pearl (surfing) = irse de punta; the board pearled = la tabla se fue de punta

period = el período; long-period swell = oleaje de período largo; short-period swell = oleaje de período corto

piece (broken) = el pedazo; there are pieces of glass everywhere = hay pedazos de vidrio por todas partes

piece (part) = la pieza; that store sells spare parts = aquella tienda vende piezas de recambio; there's a piece missing = falta una pieza pier = el muelle; it breaks on the south side of the pier = rompe al lado sur del muelle

plug (for FCS fins) = el tapón (para quillas FCS)

pocket (wave) = el hueco; the pocket is the fastest part of the wave = el hueco es la parte más rápida de la ola

pop-up = pop-up; ponerse en pie sobre la tabla

powerful = potente; very powerful = muy potente

pretty / ugly = bonito, lindo / feo; very pretty = muy bonito

price = el precio; at a good price = a buen precio; it's a good price = es un buen precio

put = poner; put it on the table = ponlo en la mesa

put on (wax, etc.) = aplicar; you put wax on the board so as not to slip = se aplica parafina a la tabla para no resbalarse

put in / take out = meter / sacar; put the board in the bag = mete la tabla dentro de la funda

put together / take apart = montar / desmontar; they took it apart and put it back together again = lo desmontaron y volvieron a montarlo

rail = el canto, el borde, el réil, el riel

rain = la lluvia; llover; it's raining hard = llueve recio; it rains a lot = llueve mucho; there's a lot of rain = hay mucha lluvia

rash guard = la lycra, la camiseta de lycra (para evitar rozaduras)

ray (fish) = la raya; at this beach there are a lot of rays = en esta playa hay muchas rayas

reach, attain: alcanzar; it doesn't reach (it's not long enough) = no alcanza; he isn't going to make it to shore = no va a alcanzar la orilla

ready = listo; I'm not ready yet = no estoy listo todavía

receipt = el recibo; you/he/she didn't give me a receipt = no me dio un recibo

reef = el arrecife, el escollo, la restinga

regular-foot = natural, normal, regular

rent = rentar, alquilar; rent a surfboard = alquilar una tabla de surf

rescue, save = rescatar, salvar; they rescued him from the rip = lo rescataron de la corriente de resaca

rescue = el rescate

resin = la resina

ride waves / ride (horse) = surfear, correr olas, navegar olas / montar, cabalgar

ride, run = correr; ride a wave = correr una ola

right / left = derecho/a / izquierdo/a; this peak is a right = este pico abre a la
    derecha
right away / in a while = en seguida / al rato
rip (surfing) = ripiar (surfear muy bien)
rip current, rip = corriente de resaca, corriente de agua que fluye hacia mar
    adentro o en paralelo a la orilla.

UNA CORRIENTE DE RESACA – VOCABULARIO

afuera = outside; el mar = the sea; liso/a = smooth; la espuma = the foam; la
rompiente = the break, the breaking wave; la dirección = the direction; la
corriente = the current; el surfista = the surfer; remontar = go (back) out;
adentro = inside; muy = very; picado/a = choppy, chopped up; uno/a = one, a;
la resaca = the backwash, rip

---

rock = la roca, la piedra, el escollo; there are rocks under the surface = hay
    rocas bajo la superficie
rough / smooth = áspero; picado (mar), revuelto (mar), bravo (mar) / liso; the
    sea is rough today = el mar está bravo hoy; the finish on this board is
    rough, not smooth = el acabado de esta tabla es áspero, no liso

run = correr

run out (all gone) = acabarse; we're out of gas = se nos acabó la gasolina

salt / salty = la sal / salado; pass the salt = pasa la sal; it's salt water, not fresh water = es agua salada, no agua dulce

same / other = mismo / otro; it's the same board = es la misma tabla; it's the same thing = es la misma cosa; es lo mismo

same, equal / different / similar = igual / diferente / parecido; it's all the same to me (I don't care) = me da igual

sand bottom = el fondo de arena

sand = la arena; a sand beach = una playa de arena

save, rescue = rescatar, salvar; the lifeguard saved my life = el salvavidas me salvó la vida

save (time, money) = ahorrar; this way we save a lot of time = así nos ahorramos mucho tiempo

screw = el tornillo; I need a screw for the fin = necesito un tornillo para la quilla; the screw won't come out = el tornillo no sale

sea / ocean = el mar / el océano

sea- = marino; sea lion = lobo marino; seaweed = alga marina; sea bed, sea floor = fondo marino, suelo marino

seagull = la gaviota

second / minute / hour = el segundo / el minuto / la hora

see = ver; I don't see it = no lo veo; you see? = ¿ves?; I don't see anything = no veo nada

sell = vender; where do they sell = dónde se vende

set = la serie, el set

shallow: there is no common Spanish word for *shallow*; you have to say "not deep" (poco profunda), "only a little water" (poca agua), etc.

shaper = shaper, persona que da forma a la tabla.

shark = el tiburón; there are a lot of sharks here = hay muchos tiburones aquí; a shark bit him = le mordió un tiburón

shin = la canilla, la espinilla; it hit me on the shin = me pegó en la canilla

shore, shoreline, beach = la orilla; the shorebreak breaks on the shore = la orillera rompe en la orilla

shorebreak = la orillera; it's hard to get past the shorebreak = es difícil pasar la orillera

short period swell / long period swell = swell de período corto / swell de período largo short / long = corto / largo; las tablas cortas miden hasta dos metros = short boards measure up to two meters [about 6'6"]

short / tall = bajo / alto; my friend is not much taller than you = mi amigo no es mucho más alto que tú

shortboard / longboard = shortboard, tabla corta / longboard, tabla larga, tablón

should = deber; I should go = debo ir; you shouldn't talk like that = no debes hablar así; you shouldn't drop in = no debes dropear

shoulder (of the wave) = el brazo (de la ola); he likes to take off on the shoulder = le gusta hacer el takeoff (arrancar) en el brazo de la ola

SERIE DE PERIODO LARGO CON VIENTO TERRAL

línea del horizonte
barco de pesca
líneas (oleaje)
rocío del viento terral
pared
surfistas remontando
espumón
corriente de resaca

SERIE DE PERÍODO LARGO CON VIENTO TERRAL – VOCABULARIO

la serie = the set; el período = the period; largo/a = long; con = with; el viento = the wind; terral = offshore; la línea = the line; el horizonte = the horizon; el barco = the boat; la pesca = fishing; el oleaje = swell; el rocío = spray, mist; la pared = the wall; el surfista = the surfer; remontar = go (back out), go back up (the face); el espumón = the whitewash, whitewater; la corriente = the current; la resaca = the backwash, rip

side = el lado; both sides = los dos lados, ambos lados

sideshore = en paralelo a la orilla, en paralelo a la costa, lateral; there's a sideshore wind = hay un viento lateral

similar / different / equal, same = parecido / diferente / igual

sink / float = hundir / flotar

size (in general) = el tamaño; what size = de qué tamaño; medium size = tamaño medio; it handles big waves = aguanta olas de gran tamaño

size (clothes, merchandise) = la talla; what size do you use? = ¿qué talla usas?

slope = la pendiente; the slope is steep = la pendiente está muy inclinada; a gentle slope = una pendiente suave

slow / fast = despacio / rápido; the waves are faster today = las olas son más rápidas hoy

slot = la ranura; the fin goes inside this slot = la quilla cabe dentro de esta ranura

small = chico, pequeño

smart, clever = listo; he's very smart = es muy listo

smooth / rough = liso / áspero, picado (mar), revuelto (mar), bravo (mar); the sea is smooth = el mar está liso; the bottom is smooth = el fondo es liso

so = tan; so big = tan grande; so expensive = tan caro; so good = tan bueno; so big = tan grande

so much = tanto; so much beer = tanta cerveza; so much money = tanto dinero

so many = tantos; so many waves = tantas olas; so many surfers = tantos surfistas

soft / hard = blando / duro

somebody, someone / nobody, no one / everybody, everyone = alguien / nadie / todos, todo el mundo

something / nothing / everything = algo / nada / todo

sometime / sometimes / always / never = alguna vez / a veces / siempre / nunca

somewhere, someplace = en algún lugar, por alguna parte

snake (surfing) = hacer una colada; he snaked me = me hizo una colada

spine (backbone) = el espinazo; (long sharp object) = la espina

spot = el spot; lugar de olas propicias para el bodyboard o el surf.

spray = la salpicadura; el rocío.

stand up, jack up = empinarse, encresparse; levantarse repentinamente la ola al encontrar un obstáculo submarino.

start / stop = empezar, comenzar / terminar, acabar; what time does it start = a qué hora empieza

start up / stop = arrancar / parar; the motor won't start = el motor no arranca; the bus stops in front of the surf shop = el autobús para delante de la tienda de surf

still / not yet / already / not anymore = todavía / todavía no / ya / ya no

stop = la parada; where is the bus stop? = ¿dónde está la parada de autobús?

steep = empinado, inclinado, vertical; it's a very steep face = es una cara muy inclinada

step on = pisar; I stepped on a stingray = pisé una raya

sting = picar; it stung me = me picó

stop / continue, keep going = parar / seguir; stop at the next corner = para en la próxima esquina; go on ahead to the next light = sigue adelante hasta el próximo semáforo

storm = la tormenta; storms create waves = las tormentas crean olas

straight = recto, derecho; keep going straight = sigue derecho

straight off, go straight off (directly toward the beach) = enfilar directamente a la playa

street = la calle; through this street = por esta calle

stringer = el alma, el nervio

strong = fuerte; there is a muy strong current = hay una corriente muy fuerte

surf forecast = el pronóstico de surf

surf report = el parte de surf

surf = surfear, correr olas

surfable, rideable = surfeable; it's rideable on a big swell = es surfeable con swell de gran tamaño

surfboard = la tabla* (*the various shapes and types are usually in English = fish, pin, gun, etc.)

surfer = el surfista; everyone are surfers = todos son surfistas

surfing (the sport) = el surf, surfear; I like surfing = me gusta surfear

swell = la marejada, el swell, el oleaje

swim = nadar; you have to swim to shore = hay que nadar hasta la orilla

tail (board or animal) = la cola; this board has a very thin tail = esta tabla tiene la cola muy fina

take = tomar; take the bus = tomar el bus; tomar el camión; take an aspirin = tomar una aspirina

take along / bring = llevar / traer; are you going to take both boards? = ¿vas a llevar las dos tablas?

take apart / put together = desmontar / montar; they took it apart and put it back together again = lo desmontaron y volvieron a montarlo

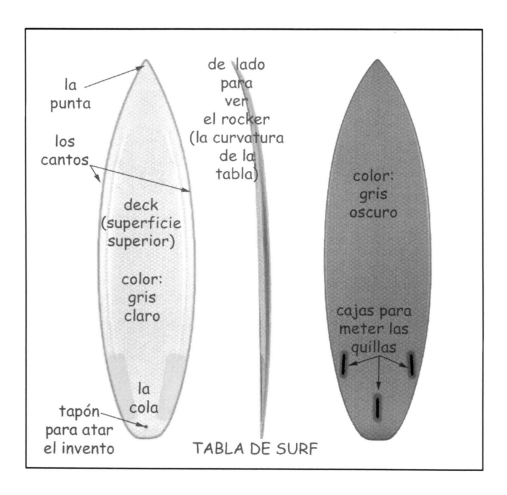

la punta

de lado para ver el rocker (la curvatura de la tabla)

los cantos

color: gris oscuro

deck (superficie superior)

color: gris claro

cajas para meter las quillas

la cola

tapón para atar el invento

TABLA DE SURF

TABLA DE SURF – VOCABULARIO

la punta = the nose (board), point, tip; el canto = the rail (board), edge; la superficie = the surface; superior = upper, superior; el color = the color; gris = gray; claro = light; la cola = the tail; el tapón = the plug; para = for; atar = to tie; el invento = the leash (surf); la tabla de surf = the surfboard; el lado = the side; ver = to see; la curvatura = the curvature; gris = gray; oscuro = dark; la caja = the box; meter = put in; la quilla = the fin (board), keel

take off, remove, take away = quitar; take off the wax = quitar la cera

take off / land (airplane) = despegar / aterrizar

take off (surf) = arrancar; I took off late = arranqué tarde; take off at an angle = arrancar en ángulo

takeoff = el arranque; good takeoff = buen arranque; steep takeoff = un arranque muy inclinado

take out / put in = sacar / meter; take your board out of the bag and let's go = saca tu tabla de la funda y nos vamos

tendon = el tendón

thank you / you're welcome = gracias / de nada, por nada, no hay de qué

that (near you) / this = eso / esto

that (over there) = aquello

there are / there aren't = hay / no hay; there aren't any waves = no hay olas

there is / there isn't = hay / no hay; there's no swell = no hay swell; there's no time = no hay tiempo; there isn't any ice = no hay hielo; are there any waves = ¿hay olas?

there / here = allí, allá / aquí; is there a surf shop around here? = ¿hay una tienda de equipo para surf por aquí?

thick / thin = grueso / delado, fino; this board is very thick = esta tabla es muy gruesa; a thick wave = una ola gruesa; the thicker the board, the higher it floats = cuanto más gruesa la tabla, más alta flota

thickness = el grosor; they sell them in various thicknesses = los venden de varios grosores

thigh = el muslo; the thigh muscle = el músculo del muslo

thin / thick = the thinner the tail, the more it sinks = cuanto más fina la cola, más se hunde

thin / fat (person) = delgado, flaco / gordo

this / that = esto / eso

throw = arrojar, lanzar, tirar; you shouldn't throw trash on the beach = no debes tirar basura en la playa

tide comes in = la marea sube

tide goes out = la marea baja

tide = la marea; high / low / medium tide = marea llena / marea seca / marea media

time (measure) = el tiempo; it's been a long time = hace mucho tiempo; there's no time = no hay tiempo time (occurrence) = la vez; sometimes yes, sometimes no = a veces sí, a veces no; I went twice = fui dos veces; this time = esta vez; the other time = la otra vez

time (of day) = la hora; ¿what time is it? = ¿qué hora es?; what time do you leave? = ¿a qué hora te vas?

tired = cansado; I'm tired = estoy cansado

to / from / until = a / de / hasta

today = hoy; if not today, tomorrow = si no hoy, mañana; there's no waves today = no hay olas hoy

toe = el dedo del pie

together / alone = juntos / solo; let's go together = vamos juntos

tomorrow = mañana; see you tomorrow = nos vemos mañana; are you going to surf tomorrow = ¿vas a surfear mañana?

toward / from = hacia / de

trade winds = los vientos alisios

trough / crest = el valle, el seno / la cresta; the height of the wave is measured from trough to crest = la altura de la ola se mide del valle a la cresta

tube = el tubo; he got a lot of tubes = cogió muchos tubos; he stayed in the tube for a long time = se quedó dentro del tubo por mucho tiempo

tunnel = el túnel

turn = el giro; a tight turn = un giro cerrado

turn = girar; you have to turn fast = hay que girar rápido; turn the handle to the left = gira la manivela hacia la izquierda

turn: it's not your turn = no te toca a ti; whose turn is it? = ¿a quién le toca?; it's my turn = me toca a mí

turtle = la cahuama, la tortuga, (surfing) hacer tortuga; to get through the wave on a longboard, you do a turtle roll = para pinchar la ola en tablón, se hace tortuga

twist = torcer; I twisted my ankle = me torcí el tobillo

ugly / pretty = feo / bonito, lindo

under = bajo, debajo de; there are rocks under the water = hay escollos bajo el agua; there's a fish under that rock = hay un pescado debajo de aquel escollo

understand = entender, comprender; I don't understand = no comprendo; understand? = ¿comprendes?

until / from / to = hasta / de / a; until later = hasta luego; until tomorrow = hasta mañana

up = arriba; up the river = río arriba; up the coast = costa arriba; farther up = más arriba

urchin = el erizo

very big / very small = muy grande / muy pequeño

very windy = hay mucho viento

very = muy

wait = esperar; wait for me at the beach = espérame en la playa; I don't like to wait = no me gusta esperar; I'm going to wait = voy a esperar

wall (house or wave) = la pared

wash / (get it) dirty = lavar / ensuciar

water = el agua; clean water = agua limpia; hot water = agua caliente; cold water = agua fría; salt water = agua salada; fresh water = agua dulce

wave = la ola; the biggest wave = la ola más grande; the biggest waves = las olas más grandes

wax = la cera, el wax, la parafina

wax = la cera; mezcla de parafina, cera de abeja e incienso, que se aplica sobre la superficie superior de la tabla para tener mayor adherencia.

weak = débil

weather = el tiempo; what's the weather = ¿qué tiempo hace?; the weather is good = hace buen tiempo

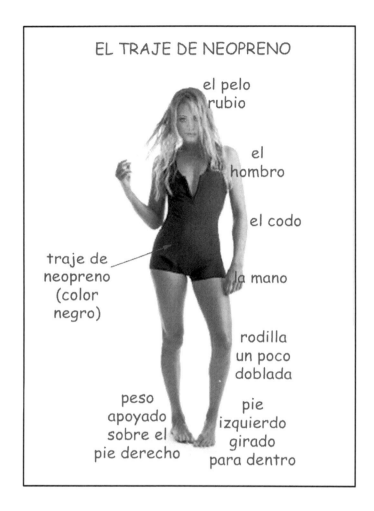

EL TRAJE DE NEOPRENO

el pelo rubio

el hombro

el codo

traje de neopreno (color negro)

la mano

rodilla un poco doblada

peso apoyado sobre el pie derecho

pie izquierdo girado para dentro

El NEOPRENO—VOCABULARIO

el traje = the suit; el neopreno = neoprene, wetsuit; el pelo = hair; rubio/a = blond; el hombro = the shoulder; el codo = the elbow; la mano = the hand; la rodilla = the knee; un poco = a little; doblado/a = bent; el pie = the foot; izquierdo/a = left (vs. right); el peso = the weight; apoyar = to support, rest on; sobre = on, over; derecho/a = right (vs. left); el color = the color; negro/a = black

week = la semana; this week = esta semana

weigh = pesar; how much does it weigh = cuánto pesa; it weighs a lot = pesa mucho; it's not so heavy = no pesa tanto

weight = el peso (in general); la pesa (for weightlifting)

welcome = bienvenido; welcome to Zihuatanejo = bienvenido a Zihuatanejo ; you're welcome = de nada, por nada, no hay de qué

wetsuit = el traje de neopreno, el neopreno

what size = ¿(de) qué tamaño? ¿(de) qué talla?; how big is it = ¿de qué tamaño es?; how big are the waves = ¿de qué tamaño son las olas?

what time = ¿(a) qué hora; what time is it = ¿qué hora es?; ¿qué horas son?; what time does it start = ¿a qué hora empieza?

what = ¿qué?

when = ¿cuándo?

where = ¿dónde?

which, which one = ¿cuál?

which, which ones = ¿cuáles?

while / during = mientras / durante

in a while = al rato; we'll leave in a while = al rato nos vamos

whitecaps = las cabrillas, los borregos = olas pequeñas, blancas y espumosas, con crestas cubiertas de espuma, que se levantan en el mar cuando este empieza a agitarse a causa del viento.

whitewater, whitewash = la espuma de la rompiente.

who = ¿quién, quiénes?; who is it = ¿quién es?; who are they = ¿quiénes son?

whose = ¿de quién?; whose is it = ¿de quién es?

why = ¿por qué?; why not = ¿por qué no?

wide = ancho; a wide beach = una playa ancha

wind swell / ground swell = mar de viento / mar de fondo

wind = el viento

windy = hay viento; it's very windy (there's a lot of wind) = hay mucho viento

with / without = con / sin; he surfs with a leash = él surfea con invento; I surf without booties = surfeo sin escarpines

work, do work = trabajar

work, function = funcionar; it works on a high tide = funciona con marea alta

worked = revolcado; I got worked = fui revolcado

worse = peor; much worse = mucho peor

worth = valer; how much is it worth = ¿cuánto vale?; it's worth the trouble = vale la pena

wrist = la muñeca

yesterday / today / tomorrow = ayer / hoy / mañana
young / old = joven / viejo
you're welcome = de nada, por nada, no hay de qué
yours = tuyo; is it yours = ¿es tuyo?

Shortcuts to expression

You can use a number of tricks to add to your linguistic firepower. A very good one—which lets you avoid the details of various verb endings and still be correct and understood—is the use of so-called auxiliary verbs: have to, want to, etc. These have the extra advantage of adding nuance and precision. You can use almost any verb (plus nouns, expressions of time, etc.) after the auxiliary verb. Here are some sample sentences:

I **have to** do it = **Tengo que** hacerlo.
I **want to** do it = **Quiero** hacerlo.
I **can** do it = **Puedo** hacerlo.
I **need to** do it = **Necesito** hacerlo.
I **should** do it = **Debo** hacerlo.
I'm **going to** do it = **Voy a** hacerlo.
I **plan to** do it = **Pienso** hacerlo.
I **know how to** do it = **Sé*** hacerlo.
It's **my turn** to do it; It's **up to me** to do it = **Me toca** hacerlo.
I **prefer** to do it = **Prefiero** hacerlo. (You can use this if you want to say "I'd rather do it.")

*sé means "I know"; it also means "I know how" in the sense that I have the knowledge or skill needed to do it. Here you can also translate as "can." (*Puedo* would mean you are able to; there is nothing preventing you.)

I know how to swim. = Sé nadar.
I can play the guitar (I know how). = Sé tocar la guitarra.
Do you know how to swim? = ¿Sabes nadar?
Can you play the piano (do you know how)? = ¿Sabes tocar el piano?

You also can say *sé cómo*, which means "I know how" in the sense that I know what way, the best way or a good way to do whatever it is; there are various possible methods and I know the one that can be used.

I know how he does that trick. = Yo sé cómo él hace ese truco.
I know you you do it, but I'd rather do it a different way. = Yo sé cómo lo haces tú, pero prefiero hacerlo de otra manera.

To say "not," "don't," "can't," etc. just put *no* before the first Spanish verb (except in the case of "prefer", where it works better <u>after</u> the verb in Spanish).

I **don't have to** do it = **No tengo que** hacerlo.
I **don't want to** do it = **No quiero** hacerlo.
I **can't** do it = **No puedo** hacerlo.
I **don't need to** do it = **No necesito** hacerlo.
I **shouldn't** do it = **No debo** hacerlo.
I'm **not going to** do it = **No voy a** hacerlo.
I **don't plan to** do it = **No pienso** hacerlo.
I **don't know how** to do it = **No sé*** hacerlo.
It's **not my turn** to do it; It's **not up to me to** do it = **No me toca** hacerlo.
I **prefer to not** do it = **Prefiero no** hacerlo. (You can use this if you want to say "I'd rather not do it.")

*no sé means "I don't know;" it also means "I don't know how" in the sense that I don't have the knowledge or skill needed to do it; I never learned how. Here you can also translate as "can't." (*No puedo* would mean you can't because something is preventing you.)

I don't know how to swim; I can't swim. = No sé nadar.
I can't play the guitar (I don't know how). = No sé tocar la guitarra.
Don't you know how to swim? = ¿No sabes nadar?
Can't you play the piano (don't you know how)? = ¿No sabes tocar el piano?

You could also say *no sé cómo*, which means "I don't know how" in the sense that I don't know what way, the best way or a good way to do whatever it is; there are various possible methods and I don't know of one that can be used.

I don't know how we're going to get there on time. = No sé cómo vamos a llegar a tiempo.
I don't know how he does it. = No sé cómo él lo hace.
I don't know how I did it, but I did it. = No sé cómo lo hice, pero lo hice.

More examples:

I don't want to go tomorrow; I'd rather go today = No quiero ir mañana; prefiero ir hoy.

I need to buy it, but I can't pay now. = Necesito comprarlo, pero no puedo pagar ahora.

I'm not going to go in the water because I can't swim. = No voy a entrar al mar porque no sé nadar.

I want to wait, but I can't. = Quiero esperar, pero no puedo.

I don't want to sell it, but I need the money. = No quiero venderlo, pero necesito el dinero.

I shouldn't do it, but I'm going to buy one more board. = No debo hacerlo, pero voy a comprar una tabla más.

I can do it today, but I'm going to wait until tomorrow. = Puedo hacerlo hoy, pero voy a esperar hasta mañana.

Notes

How to ask questions

Where is it / Where are they? = ¿Dónde está / Dónde están?
  Where's the wax? = ¿Dónde está la parafina?
  Where are the tickets? = ¿Dónde están los billetes?

Where is it (place)? = ¿Dónde queda?*
  Where's the police station? = ¿Dónde queda el cuartel de policía?
  Where's the bull ring? = ¿Dónde queda la plaza de toros?

*You also can use *dónde está*.

Where is there (one)? = ¿Dónde hay?
  Where is there a surf shop? = ¿Dónde hay una tienda de surf?
  Where is there a gas station? = ¿Dónde hay una gasolinera?

What is it / What is this / What are these? = ¿Qué es / ¿Qué es esto / Qué son éstos?

What for? = ¿Para qué?
  What is it for? = ¿Para qué sirve?
  What are they for? = ¿Para qué sirven?

Which one is it? / Which ones are they? = ¿Cuál es / ¿Cuáles son?
  Which board bag is yours? = ¿Cuál funda es la tuya?
  Which one of you dropped in on me? = ¿Cuál de ustedes me dropeó?
  Which ones do you like? = ¿Cuáles te gustan?
  Which boards are the best? =¿Cuáles tablas son las mejores?

In Spanish, *¿Cuál.../¿Cuáles...?* is often used where you would use *What...?* in English:
  What's the best beach for surfing? = ¿Cuál es la mejor playa para surfear?
  What's your name? = ¿Cuál es tu nombre?

(You might look at it this way: the literal correct answer to "what is your name" is "my name is a name." So instead of asking *what*, the question in Spanish is *which—cuál.*)

What is it like / What are they like? = ¿Cómo es / Cómo son?
    What is that beach like? = ¿Cómo es esa playa?
    What are your friends like? = ¿Cómo son tus amigos?

What time is it (now)? = ¿Qué hora es?

At what time is it (event, activity, action)? = ¿A qué hora es?
    What time is the contest? = ¿A qué hora es el concurso?
    What time is the flight? = ¿A qué hora es el vuelo?
    What time did you get here? = ¿A qué hora llegaste?

Who is it / Who are they? = ¿Quién es / Quiénes son?
    Who's that girl? = ¿Quién es aquella chica?
    Who are those guys? = ¿Quiénes son aquellos tipos?

Whose is it / Whose are they? = ¿De quién es / De quién son?
    Whose money is this? = ¿De quién es este dinero?
    Whose keys are these?= ¿De quién son estas llaves?

When is it? = ¿Cuándo es?
    When is the party? = ¿Cuándo es la fiesta?
    When is the next swell due to arrive? = ¿Cuándo debe de llegar el próximo swell?

By when? = ¿Para cuándo?
    When can you get it done by? = ¿Para cuándo lo puedes terminar?
    When do you need it by? = ¿Para cuándo lo necesitas?

How much is there? = ¿Cuánto hay?
How many are there? = ¿Cuántos hay?
    How many surfers are in the lineup? = ¿Cuántos surfistas hay en el lineup (el pico)?

How many of you are there? = ¿Cuántos son ustedes?

Why / Why not? = ¿Por qué / Por qué no?
   Why surf and not swim? = ¿Por qué surfear y no nadar?
   Why not surf and swim? = ¿Por qué no surfear y nadar?

*How are you / How are they? = ¿Cómo estás / Cómo están?
   How is the meal? = Cómo está la comida?

*For *how is it, how are you*, etc. you can use *¿Qué tal?*
   How are you? = ¿Qué tal?
   How's the food? = ¿Qué tal la comida?
   How are the waves? = ¿Qué tal las olas?
   How was the movie? = ¿Qué tal la película?
   How were the waves yesterday? = ¿Qué tal las olas ayer?
   How was it? = ¿Qué tal (fue)?

Notes

Numbers

Spanish numbers are pretty straightforward (no *"fourscore and seven"* or *"quatre-vingt-dix"* stuff).
Numbers 0-15 are individual words. So are multiples of ten (20, 30, 40, etc.), and the numbers 100, 1000 and 1,000,000 (which is written 1'000.000).
Numbers 16-99 are expressed as "10 and…" (*diez y …*) "20 and…" (*veinte y …*) "30 and…" (*treinta y …*)

1-5: uno, dos , tres, cuatro, cinco
6-10: seis, siete, ocho, nueve, diez
11-15: once, doce, trece, catorce, quince
16-19: diez y seis (dieciséis), diez y siete (diecisiete), diez y ocho (dieciocho), diez y nueve (diecinueve)

20 = veinte, 30 = treinta, 40 = cuarenta, 50 = cincuenta, 60 = sesenta, 70 = setenta, 80 = ochenta, 90 = noventa
22 = veinte y dos (veintidós); 33 = treinta y tres; 44 = cuarenta y cuatro; 55 = cincuenta y cinco
66 = sesenta y seis; 77 = setenta y siete; 88 = ochenta y ocho; 99 = noventa y nueve

100 = cien; 200 = doscientos; 300 = trescientos; 400 = cuatrocientos; 500 = quinientos
600 = seiscientos; 700 = setecientos; 800 = ochocientos; 900 = novecientos
110 = ciento diez; 125 = ciento veinte y cinco (veinticinco); 257 = doscientos cincuenta y siete

1000 = mil; 2000 = dos mil; 3000 = tres mil; 4000 = cuatro mil; etc.
10,000 = diez mil; 20,000 = veinte mil; 33,000 = treinta y tres mil; 44,000 = cuarenta y cuatro mil; etc.
100.000 = cien mil; 200,000 = doscientos mil; 350,000 = trescientos cincuenta mil; etc.
1,000,000 = un millón; 2,000,000 = dos millones; 3,300,000 tres millones trescientos mil; etc.

Notes

The calendar: Seasons, Months, Days

spring	la primavera
summer	el verano
fall, autumn	el otoño
winter	el invierno

Summer and fall are the best seasons for surfing. =
El verano y el otoño son las mejores estaciones para surfear.
In winter the ocean is very rough and in spring there is a lot of fog. =
En el invierno el mar está muy revuelto y en la primavera hay mucha niebla.

January	enero
February	febrero
March	marzo
April	abril
May	mayo
June	junio
July	julio
August	agosto
September	septiembre
October	octubre
November	noviembre
December	diciembre

I'm here until July = Estoy aquí hasta julio.
We're leaving in August = Nos vamos en agosto.
Are there good waves in March? = ¿Hay buenas olas en marzo?
April is the best month for waves = Abril es el mejor mes para olas.

Sunday	domingo
Monday	lunes
Tuesday	martes
Wednesday	miércoles
Thursday	jueves
Friday	viernes
Saturday	sábado

Are you going to the beach on Saturday? = ¿Vas a la playa el sábado?

I stay home on Saturdays. = Los sábados me quedo en casa.

The breaks are full (of people) on weekends. = Los breaks están llenos los fines de semana.

I prefer to go during the week; there are less people. = Prefiero ir durante la semana; hay menos gente.

I study on Mondays, Wednesdays and Fridays. = Los lunes, miércoles y jueves, estudio.

About the Author

Author Dave Rearwin grew up with Spanish and ended up teaching the language in a variety of settings, from American universities to a college in Japan. He also grew up surfing, made his first serious surf trip deep into mainland Mexico in the 1960s and was very glad to have the language; later trips (which featured a number of adventures that required some fast talking) made him even gladder. This book is the result of his surf travel experiences in Spanish.

Suggestions, complaints, comments: drwin808@gmail.com.